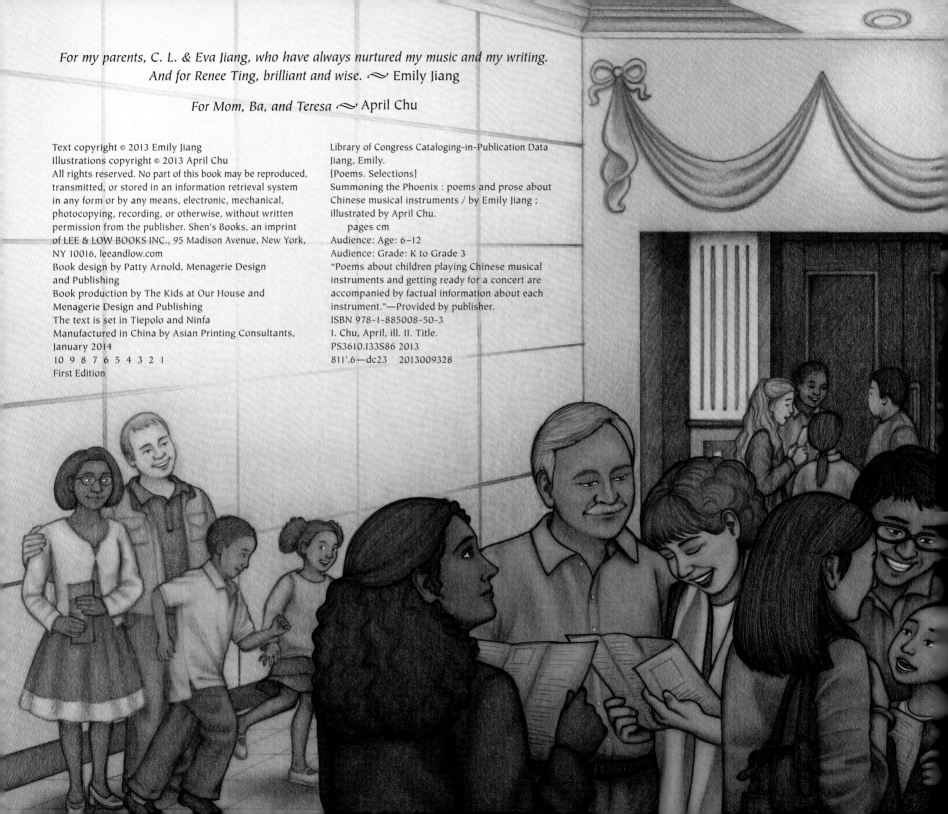

For my parents, C. L. & Eva Jiang, who have always nurtured my music and my writing.
And for Renee Ting, brilliant and wise. ∼ Emily Jiang

For Mom, Ba, and Teresa ∼ April Chu

Book design by Patty Arnold, Menagerie Design
and Publishing
Book production by The Kids at Our House and
Menagerie Design and Publishing
The text is set in Tiepolo and Ninfa
Manufactured in China by Asian Printing Consultants,
January 2014
10 9 8 7 6 5 4 3 2 1
First Edition

Library of Congress Cataloging-in-Publication Data
Jiang, Emily.
[Poems. Selections]
Summoning the Phoenix : poems and prose about
Chinese musical instruments / by Emily Jiang ;
illustrated by April Chu.
    pages cm
Audience: Age: 6–12
Audience: Grade: K to Grade 3
"Poems about children playing Chinese musical
instruments and getting ready for a concert are
accompanied by factual information about each
instrument."—Provided by publisher.
ISBN 978-1-885008-50-3
I. Chu, April, ill. II. Title.
PS3610.I33S86 2013
811'.6—dc23   2013009328

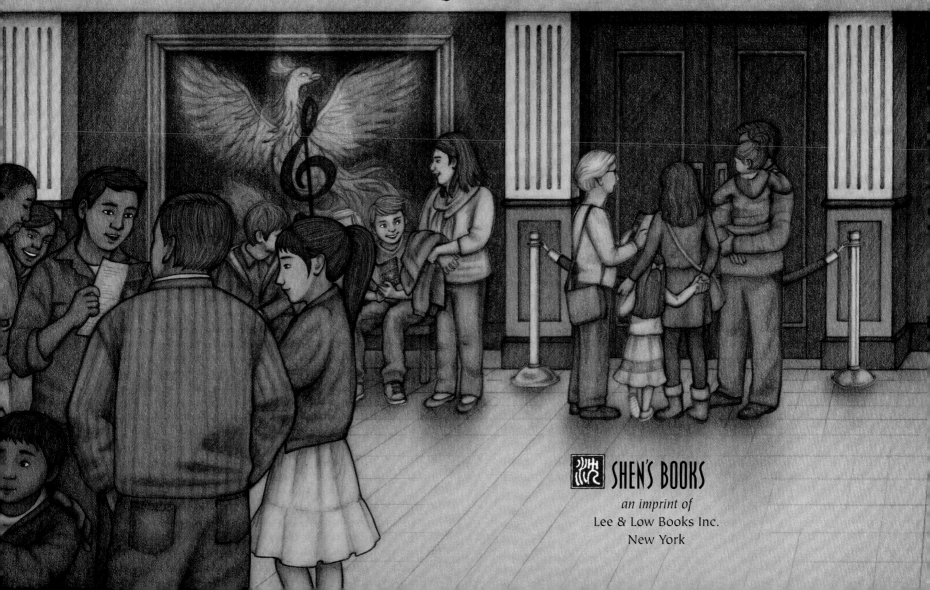

Summoning the Phoenix

Poems and Prose About Chinese Musical Instruments

BY EMILY JIANG • ILLUSTRATED BY APRIL CHU

SHEN'S BOOKS

an imprint of
Lee & Low Books Inc.
New York

Why I Chose My Erhu

When I tune my *erhu*,
I only need to listen to
Two strings. So easy!

When I play my *erhu*,
I sway from side to side
In time with my bow.

Erhu
(sounds like ur-hoo)

The *erhu* is often called the Chinese violin because both instruments have long necks, strings, and are played with bows. But the *erhu* was invented more than a thousand years ago, while the violin has only been around for a few hundred years. Although the violin has four strings, the *erhu* has just two strings. In Chinese, *er* means "two."

Unlike the violin, the bow of the *erhu* cannot be separated from the body of the instrument. The bow's strings, made of horsehair, are inserted in between the body's strings, made of metal. While the violin is played horizontally, its base tucked under the musician's chin, the *erhu* is played vertically with its base resting on the musician's lap.

In ancient times, the strings of the body of the *erhu* were made of twisted silk. Now these strings are made of steel wire, which lasts longer. The base of the *erhu* is made of wood in the shape of a hollow hexagon or octagon. While the back of the base is left open, the front is covered with stretched snakeskin. This skin vibrates at a very specific frequency and gives the *erhu* a uniquely nasal or whining sound.

When I carry my *erhu*,
I can let go of my bow—
It has nowhere to go!

Yangqin

(sounds like yang-cheen)

The *yangqin* is a stringed instrument that is not plucked or bowed, but struck by two thin, rubber-tipped bamboo sticks called hammers. Because of this, the *yangqin* is also known as the hammered dulcimer. Another name for the *yangqin* is butterfly harp. The *yangqin* came from Persia and was brought to China in the 17th century during the Ming Dynasty.

The boxy body of the *yangqin* is made of wood with raised tuning pegs and rows of wooden strips called bridges, along which the 144 strings are stretched and tuned. When it is played in performance, the *yangqin* is set on a wooden stand that is carved with geometric shapes or twin dragons.

The *yangqin* is special among Chinese instruments because its sounds are twelve-toned and chromatic (not pentatonic, which contains only five tones), and it can play the most notes, more than four octaves. Because of this and the optional foot damper pedal that mutes its sound, the *yangqin* is often used to accompany singers or other instruments.

My Place on Stage

I must play softly,
Says the conductor

Because my *yangqin* is
So much bigger (than most)

Because my *yangqin* should
Stay in the shadows

Because my *yangqin* is
Accompaniment.

But I hum the melody
When we play on stage,

And because I sit
In the center,

I imagine I am
The star.

My First Day

I arrived to rehearsal
Ten minutes late.

The conductor said,
"Your spot is here."

And pointed to the chair
Right in front!

I knocked over my stand—
Music scattered on the floor.

The conductor sighed,
"Let's get it together now."

My face warm, I nodded,
Wishing I could disappear.

"Let's breathe together now,"
Said the conductor, frowning.

Everyone played the opening
So loudly I almost

Fell off my chair. I stared
At my staff music. The notes

Swirled before me.
I did not know

Where to go.
But I breathed

With the conductor,
I listened to the sounds,

And with the next breath,
I picked up my *dizi*

And joined in.
The conductor smiled,

Then said, "Good job."
What a great first day!

Dizi
(sounds like dee-tzi)

The *dizi* is also known as the bamboo flute, although some *dizi* can be made from other kinds of wood or from stone. It is said that the *dizi* was invented by command of the Yellow Emperor who lived almost five thousand years ago. But recently someone found a *dizi* that was made eight or nine thousand years ago. It's really, really old. The original *dizi* had holes that were equidistant, or evenly spaced, along the length of the flute. This meant that the notes on the original *dizi* did not fit in a traditional scale. Now each *dizi* is made with unevenly spaced holes so that it can be played for a specific scale. Many professional *dizi* players own at least seven *dizi*, one for each scale.

The *dizi* is different from a western flute because in the middle of a *dizi* there is an extra hole. The hole is covered by a thin piece of reed that creates a loud, distinctive buzzing sound, like a kazoo. If a modern *dizi* does not have the thin reed covering the extra hole, its sound is rounder and softer. Modern *dizi* players can choose between these different kinds of sounds when performing traditional or contemporary music.

Sheng
(sounds like shung)

More than three thousand years old, the *sheng* is a mouth organ whose shape, some say, resembles the folded wings of a phoenix. The *sheng* is really a bundle of thirteen to seventeen pipes, each pipe a different length containing a reed of similar length. These pipes are connected at the base to a metal mouthpiece. To play the *sheng*, a musician presses keys near the base and blows through the mouthpiece. The breath circulates through the base and up the pipes and reeds, which make the sound. Chords can be played by covering more than one pipe. The *sheng* is unique among wind instruments because it is the only one that can harmonize with itself.

There are three sizes of *sheng*. The smallest *sheng* can be held easily in two hands and is played standing up. The middle *sheng* is typically almost three feet tall and must be played in the lap of the musician, who is sitting down. The pipes of the largest *sheng* are permanently arranged in a wooden box because the largest *sheng* is the size of a small organ.

To play a *sheng*, the musician must press her lips against the mouthpiece as if she is about to give it a kiss.

Warming Up

Before I perform,
I must warm up
my lips.

Stretch into
a smile,
a frown,
a grimace.

My favorite is
fish lips—
pucker
into a kiss.

Ew!
Not a real
kiss!

But the best way
to warm up
is to laugh:

Ha
                    Ha
        Ha!

Xiao

(sounds like shao)

Like the *dizi*, the *xiao* is thousands of years old and is made of bamboo. Unlike the *dizi*, which is played horizontally, the *xiao* is played vertically. It also plays lower notes with a much mellower tone.

There is a famous legend about the magical powers of the *xiao*. There once lived a mysterious man named Xiao Shi who loved to play the *xiao*. He played the *xiao* so beautifully that he could command the winds to move clouds and summon golden phoenixes to land nearby. He played the *xiao* at court, where he fell in love with a woman named Longyu, who liked to play the *sheng*. After they married, Longyu and her husband, Xiao Shi, often played the *sheng* and the *xiao* in harmony, and one evening their music summoned a mystical pair of a dragon and a phoenix. At that moment, Longyu learned that her husband was immortal and needed to leave the mortal world. She was faced with a difficult choice. Should she venture into the unknown with her husband or remain on earth, where it was safe? With her husband riding the dragon beside her, Longyu rode the fiery phoenix up to Heaven.

Magical Melody

Grandpa says
if I play the *xiao*
with fire
with precision
with love in the song
maybe I can
summon
a robin
a bluejay
a mockingbird

an eagle
an owl
a nightingale
a crane
a phoenix!

Suona
(sounds like soo-oh-nah)

Originating in Persia, the *suona* is thousands of years old, and it arrived in China about seventeen hundred years ago. The *suona* is made of a brass mouthpiece, a hollow wooden rod of a body, a whistle, an air plate that vibrates in the body, and a metal bowl attached at the end of the instrument. The body has seven holes along the top and one hole at the base in the back.

Traditionally the *suona* was often played at festivals since people thought it brought good luck. Because of its loud and brassy sound, it was also used in military bands and operas, as well as to accompany singers.

Originally the *suona* had finger holes like a *dizi*. But modern-day *suona* have been redesigned with keys covering the finger holes so the musicians have better control over the sound.

Friendly Competition

My best friend and I
Sit next to each other.

We play as fast as we can
Until the music turns to mush.

We play as long as we can
Until our faces turn purple-blue.

We play as loud as we can
Until the conductor yells, "Hush!"

Conquering Stage Fright

My *pipa* curves
into my lap.
It's not easy to balance
if I'm wearing a skirt
made of silk.

So I focus on the music.
Each note must be
perfectly plucked.
Each chord must be
seamlessly strummed.

Sometimes I whisper
encouraging words
to my *pipa*
so it won't slip
out of my lap.

Pipa
(sounds like pee-pah)

The *pipa* is one of the most popular Chinese instruments and is a favorite for poets to write about and to play. The *pipa* has a pear-shaped wooden body, four strings, and nineteen to twenty-six frets made of bamboo. Typically the top of the instrument is ornately decorated with an intricate carving of a flower. It is played vertically, resting on the lap of the musician. The left hand holds down the strings while the right hand plucks or strums the strings.

The traditional music of the *pipa* fits into two categories. The first category contains energetic, lively songs often inspired by great battles during war times. The second category contains mellower, gentle melodies that include rural folk songs. Because it was commonly used to play folk songs, the *pipa* is called the king of Chinese folk music.

Painting with Sound

Picking at my *guzheng*
I can feel

the crisp, clean
mountain air

breezing over
my unbound hair.

Strumming my *guzheng*
I can feel

the cold rush
of waterfall

filling my ears
with thunderous call.

Guzheng
(sounds like goo-zeng)

A popular instrument in traditional Chinese music, the *guzheng*, also known as a zither, is one of the largest stringed instruments. More than three feet long, its body is a rectangular box of wood along which are strung twenty-one to twenty-five strings. The *guzheng* rests flat on two folding wooden stands, and the musician is always seated. The sounds of a *guzheng* can evoke cascading water, horse's hooves, thunder, or landscapes.

There is a famous legend about the *guzheng*. More than two thousand years ago, a man named Yu Boya was a high-ranking officer and an accomplished musician. During his travels he often played the *guzheng* in the middle of the night. He met a woodsman named Zhong Ziyi who had heard the music and could correctly hear the images in the music: a river, a grand mountain, a simple stream growing into a waterfall. Yu Boya was amazed that Zhong Ziyi so accurately described the exact images that he saw in his head while he was playing. Because of their love of music, this high-born officer and low-born woodsman became great friends.

The Face of My Ruan

My *ruan* has two eyes
the shape of birds
flying
while I pluck
a melody.

My *ruan* has a nose
of four strings
stretching
up to the flower
carved at *ruan*'s top.

My *ruan* has no mouth,
only my arm
strumming
a chord
in harmony.

Ruan

(sounds like roo-an)

In ancient times, the *ruan* was played only during formal, official court events. Now it can be played in a variety of settings. Because of its round body, the *ruan* is often called the moon guitar.

The body of the *ruan* is made of light-colored hardwood carved with two symmetrical holes that are usually in the shape of flying birds. The back and neck and pegs of the *ruan* are made of darker-colored wood. The *ruan* is played with the base in the musician's lap while the musician presses the strings on the neck with the left hand and plucks the four strings with the right hand. There are five different sizes of *ruan*.

While the *ruan* was traditionally used to play a single melody, its four-string configuration, similar to a guitar, lends itself easily to playing harmony.

Sounds of My Muyu

My *muyu*
Sounds like
A horse
Walking.

Clip
   Clop
Clip
   Clop

My *muyu*
Sounds like
A horse
Galloping.

Clip-Clip
   Clop-Clop
Clip-Clip
   Clop-Clop

My *muyu*
Sounds like
A horse
Stopping.

Muyu
(sounds like moo-yew)

Muyu means "wooden fish." One side of the *muyu*'s hollow block is traditionally carved to resemble a fish, a symbol of wealth and good luck in Chinese culture. Several *muyu* of different sizes, and therefore different pitches, are set up in a row.

There is a legend about the *muyu*. A Buddhist traveling to India to collect sutras, or wise sayings, arrived at a vast river he could not cross. A large fish carried the Buddhist across, and the man promised to ask the Buddha to help the fish attain enlightenment. For years the man traveled around India, where he met the Buddha and gathered many sutras. Returning home, the Buddhist arrived at the same vast river, and the fish carried him again. When the fish asked about the Buddha, the man realized he had forgotten his promise. Enraged, the fish dumped the man into the river. Fortunately, he survived. Unfortunately, his sutras did not, which angered the Buddhist. He carved a fish out of a wooden block and struck it with a stick. Each time he hit the wooden fish, its mouth opened to reveal a word of a sutra. The Buddhist struck the wooden fish many, many times and recovered all his sutras.

Paigu

(sounds like pa-eye-goo)

Paigu are kettle drums, and each drum sounds a different pitch when played. The drums, usually five or six, are placed in a semicircle around the musician and are in order from the lowest to the highest pitch. The musician strikes the *paigu* using two wooden mallets.

Each drum is made of wood with animal hide stretched across the top and bottom ends. The pieces of hide are held in place by round metal frames with metal pegs that the musician can tighten or loosen to tune the pitch of the drum.

Paigu is played at the back of the orchestra because its sound is quite loud.

Keeping the Beat

The conductor says
We must always use
The metronome.

So I practice
and I count:
One - Two - Three - Four.

One and Two
and Three and
Four and . . .

I like to count
With my hands.
But in performance,

I like to listen
To the metronome
Of my heart.

Other Percussion Instruments

Luo (loo-oh)

The *luo* is a brass gong and comes in four different sizes. For the three smaller sizes, the musician holds the *luo* in one hand and strikes it with a mallet held in the other hand. The largest *luo* is almost three feet in diameter, too large to hold in one hand, and so it hangs from a frame and is struck by a large mallet.

Bo (boo-oh)

Bo are cymbals, round and made of brass. Each has a hole in the center which allows for red silk handles that the musician can wrap around his fingers. The musician holds a *bo* in each hand and plays them by striking them together.

Nanbangzi (nan-bong-tzi)

Nanbangzi is a hollow rosewood box with deep vibrating grooves. It is played with a mallet, and it rattles when struck. *Nanbangzi* was a popular instrument for operas, especially in southern China.

Bangzi (bong-tzi)

Bangzi consists of two solid rosewood sticks of different widths. *Bangzi* is played by striking the sticks together. It was used in folk music and operas in northern China.

Often, one percussionist is assigned to play all these instruments at different times during a concert.

Packing for Performance

Don't forget
My asthma inhaler
My water bottle
My snacks

Don't forget
My instruments
My music stands
My backpacks

Full of
Music scores
Concert clothes
Dress shoes
Tissue (in case
I sneeze)

But most important
Of all,

When on stage,
Don't forget
To breathe.

Being Backstage

Now I must dress up:
Shiny black shoes,
Neatly pressed concert dress
Or crisp trousers, button-down shirt,
And a bow tie
Because
Bow ties are cool.

Now I shall warm up—
Jump up and down.
Make funny faces.
Shake out my arms.
Stretch my fingers.
Keep
Everything loose.

Now I will practice . . .
My entrance: Chin up.
My stance: Sit straight.
My page turn: Flip quietly.
And especially, for the end,
How long I should take
My bow.

Because
Today
I will play . . .

In a concert!

Author's Note ～ About Chinese Music

Even though Chinese music has been played for thousands of years, the Chinese orchestra as we know it today is a modern invention less than fifty years old. It is modeled after a Western symphony orchestra, which also has been in existence for only a couple hundred years.

In ancient China, a musician performed alone or in a small band, typically with one or two instruments playing each part. These instruments were never designed to be played in a large group such as an orchestra, which often has more than five or six musicians playing the same instrument at the same time. But an orchestra can sound wonderful if every musician follows the conductor and listens carefully to match the sounds of the other musicians.

Compared to the Western chromatic scale of twelve tones or the Indian scale that has dozens of tones, the Chinese scale has only five tones. One might find Chinese music limited in what it can do. However, sometimes in the limitations, there is the opportunity for great beauty.

Chinese music will continue to evolve and adapt, while never losing the heart of its thousands-year-old tradition.

Acknowledgements

Thanks to my family and friends for their joyous support. Thanks to my wonderful SCBWI community, especially the late Sue Alexander and those involved with the Kimberly Colen Memorial Grant. Special thanks to those whose comments made my words stronger: Ann Wagner, J. L. Powers, JoAnne Wetzel. Thanks to Ellen Hopkins and Susan Hart Lindquist for helping me find April. Thanks to April for her astoundingly amazing art. And thank you, Dear Reader, for reading this book! —E.J.

Sources and Recommended Reading

Jin, Jie. *Chinese Music*. New York: Cambridge University Press, 2011.
Qiang, Xi. *Chinese Music and Musical Instruments*. Niu Jiandang, photographer, and Qiu Maoru, translator. Zurich, Switzerland: Shanghai Press, Better Link Press, 2011.